Discovering My World

D1066839

Animals in Winter

by Melvin and Gilda Berger

SCHOLASTIC INC.

New York Toronto London Auckland
Sydney Mexico City New Delhi Hong Kong

ISBN-13: 978-0-545-16079-7
ISBN-10: 0-545-16079-0

Copyright © 2010 by Melvin & Gilda Berger

All rights reserved. Published by Scholastic Inc.
SCHOLASTIC and associated logos are trademarks
and/or registered trademarks of Scholastic Inc.

12 11 10 9 8 7 6 5 4 3 2   10 11 12 13 14 15/0

Printed in the U.S.A. 40
First printing, January 2010

Where do animals go in winter?

Many bears go into dens.

They go to sleep for the winter.

Bears sometimes wake up during winter.

But then they go back to sleep.

What keeps the groundhog warm?

Groundhogs go into holes.

They sleep *without* waking, or hibernate.

Ladybugs climb plants.

Do ladybugs hibernate in groups?

Then they hibernate.

Does this bat have big wings?

Some bats fly into caves.

Then they hibernate.

Some snakes crawl under rocks.

Then they hibernate.

Ask Yourself

1. Where do many bears go in winter?
2. Do bears sleep all winter without waking?
3. Do groundhogs wake up during winter?
4. Can you name an insect that hibernates?
5. Where do some snakes hibernate?

You can find the answers in this book.